I NEVER DIED
B E F O R E

I NEVER DIED
BEFORE

EDWARD GRAY

iUniverse

I NEVER DIED BEFORE

iUniverse books may be ordered through booksellers or by contacting:

iUniverse
1663 Liberty Drive
Bloomington, IN 47403
www.iuniverse.com
844-349-9409

ISBN: 978-1-6632-3231-1 (sc)
ISBN: 978-1-6632-3232-8 (e)

Library of Congress Control Number: 2021924042

Print information available on the last page.

iUniverse rev. date: 11/24/2021

PROLOGUE

In just about seven months, I will be ninety years old!

You heard me: <u>NINETY</u> years old. About twice as old as I want to be and wanted to feel at this stage of life!

It ain't fair!

But then again, what do I have to say about it?

I do all of my exercises each and every morning and take the recommended daily walks. That at least keeps me somewhat mobile. During my last encounter with my Orthopedic Doctor, he actually said that I suffer from TMB ---- <u>T</u>oo <u>M</u>any <u>B</u>irthdays! It did not relieve the aches and pains of TMB!

If you are ancient, as I am, all of the above will not be news to you. However, I am definitely aware of it. I see it in the mirror ----- feel it in the knees ----- tire at the very beginning of a walk ---- am unsteady on getting up from a chair ---- unbalanced when upright. You get the picture, I am OLD.

In a very major sense, I am thankful that I made it at least this far.

To marry the above image with my current thinking, it finally hit me that life is not infinite in length. That's right, I will eventually die, probably in the nearer ---- as opposed to distant ----future.

As "I Have Never Died Before", I have many unanswered questions revolving around:

What to expect?

How will it happen?

How will I feel?

Will there be pain? Discomfort? Euphoria? And a Zillion other related questions.

Will I be able to communicate?

Will I be able to feed myself?

And most importantly, WHEN?

Ergo: (Yea, I can still occasionally remember the appropriate word)

It is also important to remember that Barbara (yes, she is my current and only wife of some 67 years) and I have led an extraordinary life. Barbara, the much talented and admired artist, had studied in New York City at the renowned "Art Students League" after graduating from Brooklyn College (where art luminaries such as Marc Rothko taught at the time), in Paris, London and Venice. Her paintings reside on three continents, and we lived in eight locations around the world while visiting so many others!

I was fortunate enough to have an engaging engineering and administrative career that allowed us to live on two continents and travel the world on a frequent basis.

We have no regrets as to the life we have lived to date. I just need to know a little bit more. How about the future, the how and when?

Now, why this book?

I want to record how my life progresses from this point. Physical deteriorations, ups, downs, pains, memory, etc. It is my plan to enter each and every morning for the rest of my life exactly how I feel, what new aches and pains (or lack of same) have arisen, body temperature, new medications and generally how my well-being has changed.

Each day will be a new chapter in this tome-to be!

It is for you, my reader, to review and hopefully clarify where you are on this journey.

Enjoy the rest of your life!

DAY 1

Today is the first day of the rest of my life.

Forget about each and every day being the first day of the rest of my life. A bit confusing for my first entry, however, lets get on with it.

I started to take my vital signs, beginning with my temperature, which seems to be higher than normal.

BEEP- BEEEP- BEEEEP

I then went on t
o

BEEEEEEEEEEEEEEEP!

W
h
o
o
p
s

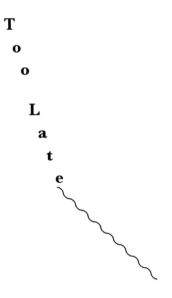

Too
Late

DAY 2

"THE BALL IS NOW IN YOUR COURT!

DAY 3

YADA-YADA-YADA

DAY 4

YADA-YADA-YADA

DAY 5

YADA-YADA-YADA

DAY 6

YADA-YADA-YADA

DAY 7

YADA-YADA-YADA

DAY 8

YADA-YADA-YADA

DAY 9

YADA-YADA-YADA

DAY 10

YADA-YADA-YADA

DAY 11

YADA-YADA-YADA

DAY 12

YADA-YADA-YADA

DAY 13

YADA-YADA-YADA

DAY 14

YADA-YADA-YADA

DAY 15

YADA-YADA-YADA

DAY 16

YADA-YADA-YADA

DAY 17

YADA-YADA-YADA

DAY 18

YADA-YADA-YADA

DAY 19

YADA-YADA-YADA

DAY 20

YADA-YADA-YADA

DAY 21

YADA-YADA-YADA

DAY 22

YADA-YADA-YADA

DAY 23

YADA-YADA-YADA

DAY 24

YADA-YADA-YADA

DAY 25

YADA-YADA-YADA

DAY 26

YADA-YADA-YADA

DAY 27

YADA-YADA-YADA

DAY 28

YADA-YADA-YADA

DAY 29

YADA-YADA-YADA

DAY 30

YADA-YADA-YADA

DAY 31

YADA-YADA-YADA

DAY 32

YADA-YADA-YADA

DAY 33

YADA-YADA-YADA

DAY 34

YADA-YADA-YADA

DAY 35

YADA-YADA-YADA

DAY 36

YADA-YADA-YADA

DAY 37

YADA-YADA-YADA

DAY 38

YADA-YADA-YADA

DAY 39

YADA-YADA-YADA

DAY 40

YADA-YADA-YADA

DAY 41

YADA-YADA-YADA

DAY 42

YADA-YADA-YADA

DAY 43

YADA-YADA-YADA

DAY 44

YADA-YADA-YADA

DAY 45

YADA-YADA-YADA

DAY 46

YADA-YADA-YADA

DAY 47

YADA-YADA-YADA

DAY 48

YADA-YADA-YADA

DAY 49

YADA-YADA-YADA

DAY 50

YADA-YADA-YADA

DAY 51

YADA-YADA-YADA

DAY 52

YADA-YADA-YADA

DAY 53

YADA-YADA-YADA

DAY 54

YADA-YADA-YADA

DAY 55

YADA-YADA-YADA

DAY 56

YADA-YADA-YADA

DAY 57

YADA-YADA-YADA

DAY 58

YADA-YADA-YADA

DAY 59

YADA-YADA-YADA

DAY 60

YADA-YADA-YADA

DAY 61

YADA-YADA-YADA

DAY 62

YADA-YADA-YADA

DAY 63

YADA-YADA-YADA

DAY 64

YADA-YADA-YADA

DAY 65

YADA-YADA-YADA

DAY 66

YADA-YADA-YADA

DAY 67

YADA-YADA-YADA

DAY 68

YADA-YADA-YADA

DAY 69

YADA-YADA-YADA

DAY 70

YADA-YADA-YADA

DAY 71

YADA-YADA-YADA

DAY 72

YADA-YADA-YADA

DAY 73

YADA-YADA-YADA

DAY 74

YADA-YADA-YADA

DAY 75

YADA-YADA-YADA

DAY 76

YADA-YADA-YADA

DAY 77

YADA-YADA-YADA

DAY 78

YADA-YADA-YADA

DAY 79

YADA-YADA-YADA

DAY 80

YADA-YADA-YADA

DAY 81

YADA-YADA-YADA

DAY 82

YADA-YADA-YADA

DAY 83

YADA-YADA-YADA

DAY 84

YADA-YADA-YADA

DAY 85

YADA-YADA-YADA

DAY 86

YADA-YADA-YADA

DAY 87

YADA-YADA-YADA

DAY 88

YADA-YADA-YADA

DAY 89

YADA-YADA-YADA

DAY 90

YADA-YADA-YADA

DAY 91

YADA-YADA-YADA

DAY 92

YADA-YADA-YADA

DAY 93

YADA-YADA-YADA

DAY 94

YADA-YADA-YADA

DAY 95

YADA-YADA-YADA

DAY 96

YADA-YADA-YADA

DAY 97

YADA-YADA-YADA

DAY 98

YADA-YADA-YADA

DAY 99

YADA-YADA-YADA

DAY 100

YADA-YAD---------

BEEEEEEEEEEEEEEEEEEP!

THE END!

Printed in the United States
by Baker & Taylor Publisher Services